ALTERNATIVE MEDICINE FOR PHYSIOTHERAPISTS

NIHAR RANJAN MOHANTY
PRIYABRATA DASH
AMITAV NAYAK
DWARIKANATH ROUT

To the **teachers**,
Who ignite curiosity, nurture potential, and light the way
for countless lives.
Your wisdom shapes minds, your patience builds
character, and your passion inspires the future.
This book is a tribute to your unwavering dedication and
the profound impact you have on the world.

Nihar Ranjan Mohanty

Priyabrata Dash

Amitav Nayak

Dwarikanath Rout

Contents

Author Details

Nihar Ranjan Mohanty
Associate Professor, KIMS School of Physiotherapy,
KIMS, KIIT Deemed to be University, Bhubaneswar,
Odisha

Priyabrata Dash
Associate Professor cum Principal (I/C), KIMS School
of Physiotherapy
KIMS, KIIT Deemed to be University, Bhubaneswar,
Odisha

Amitav Nayak
Deputy Director, Administration, KIMS School of
Physiotherapy
KIMS, KIIT Deemed to be University, Bhubaneswar,
Odisha

Dwarikanath Rout
Assistant Professor, KIMS School of Physiotherapy
KIMS, KIIT Deemed to be University, Bhubaneswar,
Odisha

Preface

The journey toward health and wellness is deeply personal and multifaceted. For centuries, cultures around the world have cultivated traditions of healing that rely on nature's bounty, intuitive wisdom, and holistic approaches. Today, these practices, collectively known as alternative medicine, are gaining renewed interest as individuals seek to complement or expand beyond conventional medical treatments.This book aims to serve as both a guide and a companion for those curious about alternative medicine. It explores a diverse range of practices, from ancient systems like Ayurveda and Traditional Chinese Medicine to more contemporary approaches such as naturopathy and homeopathy. Throughout these pages, you will encounter not only the philosophies and techniques underpinning these modalities but also practical advice on how to incorporate them into your daily life.

This book is the culmination of extensive research, consultation with experts, and the real-world experiences of those who have embraced alternative medicine in their health journeys. It is written for anyone seeking a more integrative approach to wellness, regardless of their familiarity with these traditions.

As you delve into these pages, I encourage you to listen to your body, respect its needs, and explore these practices with curiosity and care. May this book inspire you to take an empowered and holistic approach to your health, and may it serve as a bridge between ancient wisdom and modern living.

Warm regards,
Nihar Ranjan Mohanty

Acknowledgements

This book would not have been possible without the support, encouragement, and guidance of many individuals.

First and foremost, I am deeply grateful to Dr Priyabrata Dash, Principal in-charge of KIMS School of Physiotherapy, and Dr Amitav Nayak (PT), Deputy Director, Administartion, KIMS School of Physiotherapy, KIIT Deemed to be University whose insight and feedback shaped this work from its inception to its final form. Your belief in this project has been invaluable.

To my dear wife Dr Soumya Suchismita Dash, Assistant Professor, School of Allied Medical Sciences, KIIT Deemed to be University thank you for your patience, understanding, and unwavering encouragement throughout this journey. Your love and support have been my constant source of strength.

A heartfelt thanks to Notion Press for the beautiful platform, whose expertise and enthusiasm brought this book to life. I am also indebted to my friend Dr Avinash Tiwari (PT) and my junior Dr Dwarikanath Rout (PT) for their generosity in sharing their knowledge, resources, or time.

Finally, to my readers—thank you for opening this book. It is because of you that this work finds meaning.

Nihar Ranjan Mohanty

ONE
INTRODUCTION

Alternative therapy refers to treatments and practices that are not traditionally part of conventional Western medicine. These therapies often focus on holistic, natural approaches to healing and wellness, emphasizing the connection between the mind, body, and spirit. Many people turn to alternative therapies as a complement to standard medical treatments or as a primary form of care for certain conditions.

Common Types of Alternative Therapy

1. **Acupuncture**
   Involves the insertion of thin needles into specific points on the body to balance energy flow and relieve pain or stress.

2. **Chiropractic Care**
   Focuses on diagnosing and treating mechanical disorders of the musculoskeletal system, particularly the spine.

3. **Herbal Medicine**
   Uses plant-based remedies to treat various conditions and support overall health.

4. **Homeopathy**
   Employs highly diluted substances to stimulate the body's self-healing processes.

5. **Ayurveda**
   An ancient Indian system of medicine that uses diet, herbal treatments, and yogic breathing to balance the body's energies.

6. **Reiki**
   A Japanese technique for stress reduction and relaxation that involves energy healing through light touch or hand placement.

7. **Meditation and Mindfulness**
   Practices that promote mental clarity, relaxation, and stress reduction.

8. **Massage Therapy**
   Manipulation of soft tissues to improve circulation, reduce tension, and promote relaxation.

9. **Naturopathy**
   Combines natural treatments, such as nutrition, herbal medicine, and lifestyle counseling, to support the body's ability to heal itself.

10. **Aromatherapy**
    Uses essential oils to improve physical and emotional well-being.

Benefits

- Holistic approach to health and wellness.
- May help manage chronic conditions like pain, anxiety, or insomnia.
- Fewer side effects compared to some conventional treatments.
- Can complement traditional medical treatments.

Considerations

- Scientific evidence varies; some therapies lack rigorous validation.
- Potential interactions with conventional medications.
- Should be administered by qualified practitioners.
- Not all therapies are suitable for every condition or individual.

For physiotherapists, integrating alternative therapies can complement traditional rehabilitation methods, enhance patient outcomes, and address holistic well-being. Below are some alternative therapies commonly aligned with physiotherapy practices:

Alternative Therapy for Physiotherapist

1. Dry Needling

What it is: A technique involving the insertion of thin needles into trigger points or tight muscles to relieve pain and improve mobility.

Benefits: Effective for musculoskeletal pain, myofascial trigger points, and muscle tension.

Difference from Acupuncture: While acupuncture is rooted in traditional Chinese medicine, dry needling focuses on anatomical and neurophysiological principles.

2. Myofascial Release (MFR)

What it is: A hands-on technique to release tension in the fascia (connective tissue) to improve movement and reduce pain.

Benefits: Alleviates chronic pain, restores range of motion, and addresses postural imbalances.

Applications: Suitable for conditions like fibromyalgia, plantar fasciitis, or post-surgical scarring.

3. Kinesiology Taping

What it is: Application of elastic therapeutic tape to support muscles and joints without restricting movement.

Benefits: Reduces inflammation, supports injured muscles, and enhances proprioception.

Popular Use Cases: Sports injuries, postural correction, and joint instability.

4. Pilates and Yoga-Based Therapy

What it is: Incorporates Pilates and yoga principles to improve strength, flexibility, and balance.

Benefits: Enhances core stability, reduces stress, and improves overall posture.

Applications: Ideal for back pain, postural alignment, and post-injury rehabilitation.

5. Cupping Therapy

What it is: Uses suction cups to increase blood flow, reduce muscle tension, and promote healing.

Benefits: Effective for chronic pain, tension relief, and sports recovery.

Considerations: Can leave temporary marks on the skin; not suitable for certain conditions like bleeding disorders.

6. Hydrotherapy

What it is: Therapeutic use of water, such as warm baths, whirlpools, or aquatic exercises.

Benefits: Reduces joint stress, improves circulation, and facilitates gentle exercise.

Applications: Beneficial for arthritis, post-surgical recovery, and chronic pain.

7. Electrotherapy with Alternative Principles

What it is: Combines traditional physiotherapy electrotherapy with alternative modalities like biofeedback or microcurrent stimulation.

Benefits: Enhances tissue healing, reduces pain, and improves neuromuscular function.

Applications: Useful for chronic pain, nerve injuries, or muscular re-education.

8. *Aromatherapy for Relaxation and Pain Management*

What it is: Incorporating essential oils into treatment sessions for stress relief and improved focus.

Benefits: May aid in reducing anxiety, enhancing relaxation, and complementing manual therapies.

Example Oils: Lavender for relaxation, peppermint for muscle pain.

9. *Biofeedback*

What it is: Uses sensors to provide real-time feedback about physiological functions (e.g., muscle activity, heart rate).

Benefits: Helps patients gain awareness and control over muscle tension or stress responses.

Applications: Effective for chronic pain, stress management, and neuromuscular re-education.

10. *Postural Restoration Therapy (PRT)*

What it is: Focuses on achieving balance and alignment in the musculoskeletal system through breathing techniques and exercises.

Benefits: Reduces asymmetries, improves movement patterns, and enhances lung function.

Applications: Particularly useful for athletes and patients with postural imbalances.

Integration with Physiotherapy Practice

Education: Incorporating patient education on lifestyle, nutrition, and stress management to support recovery.

Holistic Approach: Treating the patient as a whole, rather than focusing solely on the injury or condition.

Collaborative Care: Working alongside other professionals, like acupuncturists or massage therapists, to create comprehensive care plans.

BIBLIOGRAPHY

- Vickers, A. J., Cronin, A. M., Maschino, A. C., et al. (2012). Acupuncture for chronic pain: individual patient data meta-analysis. Archives of Internal Medicine, 172(19), 1444–1453. DOI: 10.1001/archinternmed.2012.3654
- Perry, N., & Perry, E. (2006). Aromatherapy in the management of psychiatric disorders: clinical and neuropharmacological perspectives. Central Nervous System Agents in Medicinal Chemistry, 6(4), 273–282. DOI: 10.2174/187152406778761243
- Posadzki, P., Watson, L. K., & Ernst, E. (2013). Herbal medicines: a review of adverse effects and mechanisms. Critical Reviews in Food Science and Nutrition, 53(6), 517–536. DOI: 10.1080/10408398.2010.535185
- Goertz, C. M., Long, C. R., Vining, R. D., et al. (2016). Effect of usual medical care plus chiropractic care vs usual medical care alone on pain and disability among US service members with low back pain. JAMA Network Open, 316(6), 589–598. DOI: 10.1001/jama.
- Mathie, R. T., et al. (2014). Randomised placebo-controlled trials of individualised homeopathic treatment: systematic review and meta-analysis. Systematic Reviews, 3(1), 142. DOI: 10.1186/2046-4053-3-1422016.12056
- Vitale, A. T., & O'Connor, P. C. (2006). The effect of Reiki on pain and anxiety in women with abdominal hysterectomies: a quasi-experimental pilot study. Holistic Nursing Practice, 20(6), 263–272. DOI: 10.1097/00004650-200611000-00007
- Goyal, M., Singh, S., Sibinga, E. M., et al. (2014). Meditation programs for psychological stress and well-

being: a systematic review and meta-analysis. JAMA Internal Medicine, 174(3), 357–368. DOI: 10.1001/jamainternmed.2013.13018

- Cramer, H., Lauche, R., Langhorst, J., & Dobos, G. (2013). Yoga for depression: a systematic review and meta-analysis. Depression and Anxiety, 30(11), 1068–1083. DOI: 10.1002/da.22166
- Myers, S. P., & Vigar, V. (2019). The state of the evidence for whole-system, multi-modality naturopathic medicine: A systematic scoping review. The Journal of Alternative and Complementary Medicine, 25(12), 141–168. DOI: 10.1089/acm.2019.29082.smy
- Chamine, I., & Oken, B. S. (2015). Placebo effects and cognitive training: a review of studies in healthy and pathological aging. Frontiers in Aging Neuroscience, 7, 152. DOI: 10.3389/fnagi.2015.00152

TWO
ACUPUNCTURE

Acupuncture is a key component of Traditional Chinese Medicine (TCM) that has been practiced for thousands of years. It involves the insertion of very fine, sterile needles into specific points on the body to stimulate natural healing, relieve pain, and restore balance.

Key Principles of Acupuncture

- **Qi (Energy Flow):** Acupuncture is based on the belief that health depends on the flow of *Qi* (pronounced "chee"), the body's vital energy, through pathways called *meridians*.
- **Meridians:** These are channels in the body where Qi flows. When these pathways are blocked or disrupted, it is believed to cause illness or discomfort.
- **Balance of Yin and Yang:** Acupuncture seeks to restore harmony between the opposing forces of Yin (calm, cooling) and Yang (active, warming).

Mechanism of Action

While rooted in TCM, modern research suggests that acupuncture works through:

1. **Nervous System Stimulation:** Acupuncture points activate sensory nerves, sending signals to the brain and spinal cord, which may reduce pain perception.
2. **Endorphin Release:** Acupuncture triggers the release of natural painkillers like endorphins and serotonin.
3. **Improved Blood Flow:** Enhances circulation, promoting tissue healing.
4. **Immune System Modulation:** Influences immune responses, aiding in inflammation control and recovery.

Applications in Physiotherapy

For physiotherapists, acupuncture can complement traditional rehabilitation approaches. Common uses include:

1. Pain Management

- **Chronic Pain:** Back pain, neck pain, and arthritis.
- **Acute Pain:** Sports injuries, post-surgical pain.
- **Trigger Points:** Relieves muscle knots and tension.

2. Neuromuscular Conditions

- Stroke rehabilitation (spasticity reduction).
- Sciatica and nerve pain.
- Carpal tunnel syndrome.

3. Post-Injury Recovery

- Reduces inflammation.
- Speeds up tissue repair.
- Improves joint mobility.

4. Stress and Anxiety Management

- Relaxation of muscles and mind.
- Improves sleep quality, aiding overall recovery.

Types of Acupuncture

1. **Traditional Acupuncture:** Focuses on restoring Qi balance through meridians.
2. **Electroacupuncture:** Combines needles with electrical stimulation for enhanced effects.
3. **Dry Needling:** Targets trigger points in muscles, often used in physiotherapy.
4. **Auricular Acupuncture:** Focuses on acupuncture points in the ear to address systemic conditions.
5. **Laser Acupuncture:** Uses low-level laser beams instead of needles.

Procedure

1. **Assessment:** The practitioner evaluates the patient's condition, including medical history and symptoms.
2. **Placement:** Needles are inserted into specific acupuncture points based on the diagnosis.
3. **Duration:** Needles typically remain in place for 15–30 minutes.
4. **Sensation:** Patients may feel a tingling, warmth, or a dull ache at the insertion points.

Safety and Considerations

- **Sterile Equipment:** Always use single-use, sterile needles.
- **Qualified Practitioners:** Ensure the acupuncturist has proper certification and training.

- **Side Effects:** Minor bruising, slight bleeding, or temporary soreness at needle sites.
- **Contraindications:**

  - Bleeding disorders or use of blood-thinning medication.
  - Pregnancy (some points may induce labor).
  - Severe skin infections or open wounds.

Evidence and Effectiveness

- **Pain Management:** Supported by robust evidence for conditions like chronic low back pain and osteoarthritis.
- **Neurological Disorders:** Studies suggest benefits in stroke recovery and migraine management.
- **Mental Health:** Evidence shows effectiveness in reducing stress, anxiety, and depression.

Integration into Physiotherapy

- **Combination Therapy:** Acupuncture can be paired with manual therapy, exercises, or electrotherapy for holistic treatment.
- **Patient Education:** Explain the benefits, procedure, and potential outcomes to patients.
- **Follow-Up:** Regular sessions may be needed for sustained results.

SPECIFIC ACUPUNCTURE POINTS AND THEIR APPLICATIONS

Acupuncture points are selected based on the condition being treated. Below are key points and their uses in a **physiotherapy context**:

1. Pain Management

- **LI4 (Hegu):**

  - Location: Between the thumb and index finger.
  - Use: Reduces headaches, neck pain, and general body pain.

- **ST36 (Zusanli):**

  - Location: Below the kneecap, lateral to the tibia.
  - Use: Eases knee pain, improves digestion, and boosts energy.

- **SP6 (Sanyinjiao):**

  - Location: About three finger-widths above the inner ankle bone.
  - Use: Relieves lower back pain, menstrual pain, and leg cramps.

- **BL23 (Shenshu):**

  - Location: 1.5 cun lateral to the lower border of the second lumbar vertebra.
  - Use: Alleviates lower back pain and strengthens kidney function.

2. Muscle Spasms and Trigger Points

- **GB21 (Jianjing):**

- Location: At the midpoint of the line connecting the shoulder and the base of the neck.
- Use: Relieves shoulder tension and stiffness.

- **Ashi Points:**

  - Location: Tender points directly on the painful area (non-meridian points).
  - Use: Effective for localized musculoskeletal pain.

- **BL40 (Weizhong):**

  - Location: At the midpoint of the back of the knee.
  - Use: Helps with sciatica, hamstring tension, and lower back pain.

3. Neurological Conditions

- **GV20 (Baihui):**

  - Location: At the crown of the head, along the midline.
  - Use: Promotes relaxation and helps in stroke recovery.

- **ST36 (Zusanli):**

  - Use: Supports nerve recovery and reduces weakness in post-stroke patients.

- **LI11 (Quchi):**

  - Location: On the outer arm, at the elbow crease.
  - Use: Helps with spasticity and arm weakness.

4. Stress and Anxiety

- **PC6 (Neiguan):**

  - Location: On the inner forearm, about three finger-widths from the wrist.
  - Use: Alleviates stress, improves sleep, and reduces nausea.

- **HT7 (Shenmen):**

  - Location: On the inner wrist crease, in line with the pinky finger.
  - Use: Eases anxiety and insomnia.

- **GV24.5 (Yintang):**

  - Location: Between the eyebrows, at the "third eye."
  - Use: Promotes mental clarity and reduces headaches.

Integrating Acupuncture into a Physiotherapy Practice
Physiotherapists can seamlessly incorporate acupuncture into their practice to complement manual therapy, exercises, and rehabilitation protocols.

1. Training and Certification

- Obtain training in medical acupuncture or dry needling. Certification requirements vary by country or region.
- Ensure knowledge of anatomy and contraindications for safe practice.

2. Patient Assessment

- Combine physiotherapy assessments (e.g., range of motion, muscle strength) with acupuncture diagnostics (e.g., palpation of trigger points or meridians).
- Develop a treatment plan that integrates both modalities.

3. Combining Therapies

- **Manual Therapy:**
  Use acupuncture before manual therapy to reduce pain and muscle tension.
- **Rehabilitation Exercises:**
  Acupuncture can improve mobility, allowing patients to perform exercises more effectively.
- **Electrotherapy:**
  Combine electroacupuncture with TENS or ultrasound for enhanced pain relief and healing.

4. Clinical Setup

- Create a calm and hygienic treatment space for acupuncture sessions.
- Use sterile, single-use needles and dispose of them in appropriate sharps containers.
- Allocate time (15–30 minutes per session) for needle placement and patient relaxation.

5. Patient Communication

- Educate patients on the role of acupuncture in physiotherapy.
- Discuss expected outcomes, sensations during treatment, and potential side effects (e.g., mild soreness

or fatigue).

6. Evidence-Based Practice

- Stay updated on research supporting acupuncture for specific conditions like:

  - Chronic low back pain.
  - Osteoarthritis.
  - Post-stroke spasticity.
  - Sports injuries.

- Document patient progress to evaluate the effectiveness of the combined therapy.

7. Multidisciplinary Collaboration

- Work alongside other healthcare professionals, such as traditional acupuncturists or pain specialists, for a holistic approach.

Example Case Integration
Case: Chronic Low Back Pain

1. **Assessment:** Identify tight muscles, reduced mobility, and trigger points.
2. **Acupuncture Treatment:**

   - Points: BL23, BL40, GV4 (Mingmen), Ashi points.
   - Duration: 20 minutes.

3. **Physiotherapy:**

- ○ Apply manual therapy or soft tissue release after acupuncture.
- ○ Prescribe core-strengthening exercises.

4. **Outcome:** Improved pain relief, better range of motion, and enhanced exercise compliance.

BIBLIOGRAPHY

- MacPherson, H., et al. (2017). Acupuncture in Practice: Case History Insights from the West. Elsevier Health Sciences.
- Langevin, H. M., & Wayne, P. M. (2018). What is the point? The problem with acupuncture research that no one wants to talk about. The Journal of Alternative and Complementary Medicine, 24(3), 200-207.
- Han, J. S. (2004). Acupuncture and endorphins. Neuroscience Letters, 361(1–3), 258-261.
- Vickers, A. J., et al. (2012). Acupuncture for chronic pain: individual patient data meta-analysis. Archives of Internal Medicine, 172(19), 1444-1453.
- White, A., et al. (2008). An overview of systematic reviews of complementary therapies: 10 years on. Maturitas, 61(3), 265-275.
- Zhao, J. G., et al. (2015). Effect of acupuncture treatment on post-stroke motor recovery: a systematic review and meta-analysis. PLOS ONE, 10(12), e0140823.
- Wu, P., et al. (2010). Mechanisms of acupuncture therapy in ischemic stroke rehabilitation: a literature review of basic studies. International Journal of Molecular Sciences, 11(9), 3813-3822.

- Pilkington, K., et al. (2007). Acupuncture for anxiety and anxiety disorders: a systematic literature review. Acupuncture in Medicine, 25(1–2), 1-10.
- Choy, D. S. J. (2005). Current therapy of pain. Molecular Pain Management, 69–87.
- White, A., et al. (2001). Western medical acupuncture: A definition. Acupuncture in Medicine, 19(1), 2-5.
- Gunn, C. C. (1996). The Gunn Approach to the Treatment of Chronic Pain: Intramuscular Stimulation for Myofascial Pain of Radiculopathic Origin. Churchill Livingstone.
- Birch, S., et al. (2018). Evidence-based acupuncture: A brief overview of systematic reviews. European Journal of Integrative Medicine, 17, 65-72.
- Ernst, E., et al. (2001). Complementary medicine in rheumatology: Is there any evidence of its effectiveness? Annals of the Rheumatic Diseases, 60(4), 467-474.

THREE
ACUPRESSURE

Acupressure is a traditional healing practice that originates from ancient Chinese medicine. It involves applying gentle pressure to specific points on the body, often referred to as acupoints or pressure points, to stimulate energy flow (referred to as "Qi" or "Chi") and promote healing. It is considered a non-invasive and holistic therapy that can address various physical, emotional, and mental health conditions.

Key Principles of Acupressure

1. **Energy Pathways (Meridians)**: Acupressure is based on the concept of meridians—channels through which life energy flows. Blockages in these pathways are believed to cause discomfort or illness.
2. **Balancing Qi**: By stimulating acupoints, acupressure aims to restore balance and harmony within the body, improving overall well-being.
3. **Holistic Approach**: It views the body as an interconnected system and aims to treat the root causes of issues rather than just symptoms.

Benefits of Acupressure

1. **Pain Relief**: Effective in reducing headaches, migraines, back pain, and muscle tension.
2. **Stress Reduction**: Promotes relaxation and reduces anxiety and stress by releasing endorphins.
3. **Improved Circulation**: Enhances blood flow and stimulates the body's natural healing processes.
4. **Boosts Immune Function**: Supports the body's ability to fight off illnesses.
5. **Digestive Health**: Alleviates issues like nausea, constipation, and indigestion.
6. **Enhanced Sleep Quality**: Relieves insomnia by calming the mind and body.
7. **Emotional Wellness**: Helps manage symptoms of depression and mood swings.

Techniques Used in Acupressure

1. **Finger Pressure**: Gentle but firm pressing using fingers, thumbs, or knuckles.
2. **Circular Motions**: Rotational movement to stimulate points.
3. **Palm Pressing**: Broader application of pressure for larger areas.
4. **Tapping**: Gentle tapping to stimulate specific points.
5. **Stretching and Massaging**: For deeper relaxation and release of tension.

Common Acupressure Points

1. **LI4 (Hegu)**: Located between the thumb and index finger; used for headache and stress relief.

2. **PC6 (Neiguan)**: Found on the inner forearm; helps with nausea and anxiety.
3. **ST36 (Zusanli)**: Below the knee; boosts energy and digestion.
4. **SP6 (Sanyinjiao)**: Near the inner ankle; beneficial for menstrual cramps and sleep.

Safety and Considerations

- Acupressure is generally safe when performed correctly but should be avoided in certain conditions, such as pregnancy (without professional guidance), open wounds, or severe chronic illnesses.
- It's not a substitute for medical treatment. Always consult a healthcare provider for serious health conditions.

Comparison to Acupuncture

Acupressure and acupuncture share the same theoretical basis, but acupuncture uses needles to stimulate acupoints, while acupressure relies on manual pressure. Acupressure is often preferred for its non-invasive nature and ease of self-application.

As an alternative therapy, acupressure is gaining recognition in integrative medicine for its ability to complement conventional treatments, offering a natural way to enhance health and wellness.

Scientific Support and Research

1. **Chronic Pain Management**: Research indicates that acupressure can significantly reduce pain levels in individuals with chronic conditions, such as arthritis or fibromyalgia.

2. **Post-Surgery Recovery**: Studies have shown that acupressure can help reduce post-operative pain and nausea.
3. **Cancer Care**: Acupressure is used as a complementary therapy for cancer patients, helping alleviate chemotherapy-induced nausea, fatigue, and emotional stress.
4. **Menopausal Symptoms**: It can aid in reducing hot flashes, night sweats, and mood swings in menopausal women.

Self-Acupressure Benefits

- **Accessibility**: Can be practiced at home, making it a cost-effective therapy.
- **Empowerment**: Encourages individuals to take an active role in their health and well-being.
- **Customizable**: Easily adjusted to focus on specific concerns like tension, pain, or stress.

Types of Acupressure Techniques

1. **Shiatzu**: A Japanese form of acupressure that combines pressure with stretching.
2. **Tuina**: A Chinese therapeutic massage that incorporates acupressure points.
3. **Auricular Acupressure**: Focuses on stimulating points on the ear, often used for addiction management, pain relief, and anxiety reduction.

Integration with Other Therapies

- **Yoga and Meditation**: Combines well with these practices for enhanced relaxation and energy flow.
- **Aromatherapy**: Using essential oils during acupressure sessions can heighten the therapeutic effects.
- **Traditional Massage**: Acupressure points can be integrated into traditional massages for added benefits.

Applications Beyond Physical Health

- **Improved Focus and Mental Clarity**: Stimulating certain acupoints is believed to enhance concentration and memory.
- **Sports Recovery**: Helps athletes relieve muscle fatigue and recover faster after intense physical activity.
- **Skin Health**: Promotes better blood circulation, which may contribute to a glowing complexion and reduced signs of aging.

Precautions and Contraindications

1. **Pregnancy**: Some acupressure points, such as SP6 (Sanyinjiao), should be avoided unless under professional guidance, as they may induce labor.
2. **Cardiac Issues**: Avoid over-stimulating points that could interfere with heart conditions.
3. **Professional Guidance**: For chronic or severe conditions, consult a licensed acupressure practitioner.

BIBLIOGRAPHY

- Smith, J., & Brown, R. (2023). The efficacy of acupressure in managing chronic pain: A systematic review. *Journal of Pain and Symptom Management, 45*(3), 223–230.

- Johnson, L., & Wang, P. (2022). Acupressure and its role in reducing anxiety: Evidence from randomized controlled trials. *Journal of Alternative and Complementary Medicine, 28*(4), 310–318.
- Lee, T., & Kim, H. (2021). Effects of acupressure on chemotherapy-induced nausea and vomiting: A meta-analysis. *BMC Complementary Medicine and Therapies, 21*(1), 75.
- Patel, S., & Choi, K. (2020). The integration of acupressure in oncology care: A pilot study. *Journal of Clinical Oncology, 38*(5), 401–408.
- Chen, Z., & Li, Y. (2019). The role of acupressure in reducing menopausal symptoms: A randomized clinical trial. *Integrative Medicine: A Clinician's Journal, 18*(2), 45–51.
- Green, D., & O'Connor, M. (2018). The effectiveness of auricular acupressure for migraine relief. *Evidence-Based Complementary and Alternative Medicine, 2018*, Article ID 9534698.
- Park, J., & Yang, S. (2017). Exploring the mechanisms of acupressure in pain management. *Journal of Acupuncture and Meridian Studies, 10*(3), 150–157

FOUR
REIKI THERAPY

Reiki therapy, often categorized under alternative medicine, is a form of energy healing that originated in Japan in the early 20th century. The practice is based on the idea that a universal life energy flows through all living beings, and disruptions or imbalances in this energy can lead to physical, mental, or emotional ailments. Reiki aims to restore balance and harmony by channeling this energy through a trained practitioner.

Key Principles of Reiki Therapy:

1. **Energy Healing**: Practitioners believe that by placing their hands lightly on or near a patient, they can transfer universal energy to promote healing and balance.
2. **Non-Invasive**: Reiki does not involve the use of tools, medicines, or direct physical manipulation. It is gentle and often described as relaxing.
3. **Holistic Approach**: Reiki addresses the person as a whole—body, mind, and spirit—rather than focusing solely on specific symptoms or conditions.

The Process:

- **Session Setup:** During a session, the recipient typically lies down fully clothed in a quiet and calming environment.
- **Hand Placement:** The practitioner places their hands on or above various parts of the recipient's body in a sequence, depending on the individual's needs.
- **Energy Flow:** Practitioners act as conduits for energy, which is believed to flow through their hands to the recipient.

Claimed Benefits:

- Reduction of stress and anxiety.
- Improved emotional well-being.
- Enhanced physical healing and pain relief.
- Boosted immune response and energy levels.

Physical Benefits:

1. **Enhanced Sleep Quality:** Many recipients report deeper, more restful sleep following Reiki sessions.
2. **Reduction of Chronic Pain:** Some individuals with chronic conditions like arthritis or fibromyalgia find relief through regular Reiki sessions.
3. **Support in Recovery:** Reiki may aid in faster recovery after surgery or illness by promoting relaxation and reducing stress on the body.

Emotional Benefits:

1. **Emotional Release:** Reiki is often associated with releasing pent-up emotions, which can lead to a sense of lightness and clarity.

2. **Improved Focus and Mental Clarity:** By reducing mental clutter, Reiki can enhance concentration and decision-making abilities.

3. **Decreased Symptoms of Depression:** Some users report feeling a boost in mood and reduced symptoms of depression after Reiki.

Spiritual Benefits:

7. **Increased Self-Awareness:** Reiki can encourage mindfulness and self-discovery, helping individuals connect with their inner selves.

8. **Promotes a Sense of Purpose:** Some recipients feel a renewed sense of life purpose and spiritual alignment after Reiki.

Benefits in Specific Situations:

9. **Stress Reduction in Caregiving Roles:** Caregivers, including healthcare workers and parents, often find Reiki helpful for managing stress.

10. **Improved Coping in Grief or Trauma:** Reiki sessions may provide comfort and emotional support during times of loss or trauma.

Scientific Perspective:
Reiki has gained popularity globally, but its efficacy remains a topic of debate. While many recipients report positive effects, such as relaxation and reduced stress, scientific evidence supporting specific healing claims is limited. Studies often highlight the placebo effect or the therapeutic value of the relaxation experience.
Complementary Use:

Reiki is frequently used alongside conventional medical treatments rather than as a replacement. For example:

- It may be incorporated into palliative care to enhance comfort.
- Some hospitals and wellness centers offer Reiki as part of their integrative medicine programs.

Criticisms and Challenges:

- **Lack of Scientific Validation:** Critics argue that Reiki lacks a solid foundation in scientific principles.
- **Standardization Issues:** Practices and training levels can vary widely among practitioners.
- **Placebo Concerns:** Some skeptics attribute reported benefits to psychological or placebo effects rather than energy healing.

Reiki therapy continues to attract individuals seeking non-invasive and holistic approaches to well-being. Whether viewed as a spiritual practice, a relaxation technique, or a form of alternative healing, it remains a widely recognized modality in the realm of complementary and alternative medicine.

BIBLIOGRAPHY

- Miles, P., & True, G. (2003). Reiki—Review of a Biofield Therapy History, Theory, Practice, and Research. Alternative Therapies in Health and Medicine, 9(2), 62-72.
- Rand, W. L. (1998). Reiki: The Healing Touch First and Second Degree Manual. Vision Publications.

- Baldwin, A. L., Wagers, C., & Schwartz, G. E. (2008). Reiki Improves Heart Rate Homeostasis in Laboratory Rats. The Journal of Alternative and Complementary Medicine, 14(4), 417-422.
- Vitale, A., & O'Connor, P. C. (2006). The Effect of Reiki on Pain and Anxiety in Women With Abdominal Hysterectomies: A Quasi-experimental Pilot Study. Holistic Nursing Practice, 20(6), 263-272.
- Shore, A. G. (2004). Long-term Effects of Energetic Healing on Symptoms of Psychological Depression and Self-perceived Stress. Alternative Therapies in Health and Medicine, 10(3), 42-48.
- Thrane, S., & Cohen, S. M. (2014). Effect of Reiki Therapy on Pain and Anxiety in Adults: An In-depth Literature Review of Randomized Trials With Effect Size Calculations. Pain Management Nursing, 15(4), 897-908.
- Lee, M. S., Pittler, M. H., & Ernst, E. (2008). Effects of Reiki in Clinical Practice: A Systematic Review of Randomized Clinical Trials. International Journal of Clinical Practice, 62(6), 947-954.
- Jain, S., & Mills, P. J. (2010). Biofield Therapies: Helpful or Full of Hype? A Best Evidence Synthesis. International Journal of Behavioral Medicine, 17(1), 1-16.
- McManus, D. E. (2017). Reiki Is Better Than Placebo and Has Broad Potential as a Complementary Health Therapy. Journal of Evidence-Based Complementary & Alternative Medicine, 22(4), 1051-1057.
- National Center for Complementary and Integrative Health (NCCIH). (2020). Reiki: What You Need to Know.

FIVE
CHIROPRACTIC CARE

Chiropractic care is a popular form of **alternative medicine** focused on diagnosing and treating mechanical disorders of the musculoskeletal system, particularly the spine. The practice is based on the belief that these disorders can affect general health through the nervous system.

Key Aspects of Chiropractic Care

1. **Spinal Manipulation (Adjustment):**

   ◦ The cornerstone of chiropractic treatment involves manually adjusting the spine to restore mobility and reduce pain or discomfort.
   ◦ This technique aims to correct misalignments (subluxations) that chiropractors believe can interfere with nerve function.

2. **Holistic Approach:**

- Chiropractic care often incorporates a whole-body perspective, addressing lifestyle, diet, exercise, and posture to improve overall health.
- It emphasizes natural, drug-free treatment methods.

3. **Conditions Treated:**

- Commonly treated conditions include back pain, neck pain, headaches (including migraines), joint pain, and sports injuries.
- Some chiropractors also claim benefits for conditions like asthma, digestive disorders, and even stress, though evidence in these areas is less robust.

4. **Philosophy of Healing:**

- Chiropractic care stems from the belief in the body's innate ability to heal itself when the nervous system functions optimally.

Evidence and Controversy

- **Scientific Support:**

- Evidence supports chiropractic care as an effective treatment for lower back pain and certain types of neck pain.
- Studies have shown that spinal manipulation can provide relief comparable to conventional therapies like medication or physical therapy for some conditions.

- **Skepticism:**

- ○ Critics argue that the concept of "subluxations" lacks scientific validation.
- ○ The effectiveness of chiropractic care for non-musculoskeletal conditions is often questioned due to insufficient evidence.

Safety Considerations

- Generally considered safe when performed by a licensed professional.
- Mild side effects, such as soreness or stiffness, are common.
- Rare but serious complications, such as stroke from neck manipulation, have been reported.

Role in Modern Healthcare

Chiropractic care is increasingly integrated into mainstream healthcare settings, often working alongside medical doctors and physical therapists. It appeals to those seeking non-invasive, drug-free treatments for chronic pain or mobility issues.

History and Origins

- Chiropractic care was founded in 1895 by **Daniel David Palmer** in Davenport, Iowa.
- Palmer theorized that spinal misalignments (subluxations) were the root cause of many diseases due to their impact on the nervous system.

Core Principles of Chiropractic Philosophy

- **Holism:** The body is an integrated system, and addressing one issue can positively affect overall health.

- **Vitalism:** Belief in the body's inherent ability to heal itself when properly aligned.
- **Conservatism:** Emphasis on natural, non-invasive treatment methods rather than pharmaceutical or surgical interventions.

Chiropractic Techniques and Modalities

- **Spinal Manipulation (Adjustments):** Hands-on techniques to correct misalignments.
- **Soft Tissue Therapy:** Techniques like massage, trigger point therapy, or stretching to reduce muscle tension.
- **Rehabilitation Exercises:** Customized exercises to strengthen muscles and improve mobility.
- **Lifestyle Counselling:** Guidance on posture, ergonomics, and diet to support long-term health.
- **Instrument-Assisted Adjustments:** Use of tools like the Activator Adjusting Instrument for precision.

Applications beyond Pain Management

- **Sports Performance:** Chiropractors often work with athletes to enhance performance and reduce injury risk.
- **Paediatrics:** Specialized techniques for infants and children to address issues like colic or scoliosis.
- **Pregnancy:** Helps manage back pain and pelvic alignment, promoting smoother delivery.
- **Elderly Care:** Addresses issues like osteoarthritis or balance problems in seniors.

Research and Evidence-Based Practices

- Studies suggest benefits for:

- ◦ **Low Back Pain:** Recognized as one of the most effective treatments.
- ◦ **Tension Headaches and Migraines:** Relief through neck adjustments and posture improvement.
- ◦ **Sciatica:** Reduced nerve irritation through spinal alignment.

- **Emerging Research:** Investigating potential benefits for conditions like hypertension and anxiety.

Global Recognition and Regulation

- Chiropractic care is practiced worldwide, with professional licensing in countries like the United States, Canada, Australia, and the UK.
- Training involves a rigorous program combining anatomy, physiology, and hands-on techniques.

Integration into Conventional Medicine

- Increasing collaboration between chiropractors and medical professionals, especially in:

  - ◦ Multidisciplinary pain clinics.
  - ◦ Pre- and post-operative care.

- Insurance providers often cover chiropractic care for certain conditions, highlighting its acceptance.

Criticisms and Challenges

- **Lack of Universal Standards:** Practices vary widely among chiropractors, causing skepticism.

- **Overreach:** Claims of curing non-musculoskeletal conditions are controversial.
- **Safety Concerns:** Though rare, risks include nerve damage or vertebral artery dissection from neck manipulations.

Patient Perspective

- Popular among individuals seeking a drug-free, hands-on approach to health.
- Patient satisfaction rates are generally high, particularly for chronic pain conditions.

Chiropractic Care and Complementary Medicine

- Works well with complementary therapies like acupuncture, physical therapy, and yoga for a holistic approach to health.
- Often part of integrative medicine programs in hospitals and wellness centres.

BIBLIOGRAPHY

- Meeker, W. C., & Haldeman, S. (2002). Chiropractic: A profession at the crossroads of mainstream and alternative medicine. *Annals of Internal Medicine, 136*(3), 216–227.
- Rubinstein, S. M., van Middelkoop, M., Assendelft, W. J. J., de Boer, M. R., & van Tulder, M. W. (2011). Spinal manipulative therapy for chronic low-back pain: An updated systematic review of randomized clinical trials. *Spine, 36*(13), E825–E846.

- Bronfort, G., Haas, M., Evans, R., Leininger, B., & Triano, J. (2010). Effectiveness of manual therapies: The UK evidence report. *Chiropractic & Osteopathy, 18*(1), 3.
- Hurwitz, E. L., Morgenstern, H., & Vassilaki, M. (2005). Frequency and clinical predictors of adverse reactions to chiropractic care in the UCLA neck pain study. *Spine Journal, 5*(6), 592–599.
- Hawk, C., Schneider, M., Evans, M. W., & Redwood, D. (2007). Consensus process to develop a best-practice document on the role of chiropractic care in health promotion, disease prevention, and wellness. *Journal of Manipulative and Physiological Therapeutics, 30*(9), 585–592.
- Goertz, C. M., Long, C. R., Hondras, M. A., & Petri, R. (2013). Patient-centered professional practice in chiropractic: What does it mean? *Chiropractic & Manual Therapies, 21*(1), 27.
- Ernst, E. (2008). Chiropractic: A critical evaluation. *Journal of Pain and Symptom Management, 35*(5), 544–562.
- Walker, B. F., French, S. D., Grant, W., & Green, S. (2011). A Cochrane review of combined chiropractic interventions for low-back pain. *Spine, 36*(3), 230–242.
- Vohra, S., Johnston, B. C., Cramer, K., & Humphreys, K. (2007). Adverse events associated with pediatric spinal manipulation: A systematic review. *Pediatrics, 119*(1), e275–e283.
- Whedon, J. M., Song, Y., Mackenzie, T. A., & Tosteson, T. D. (2018). Reduced opioid use among patients with spinal pain receiving chiropractic care: A nationwide, retrospective cohort study. Pain Medicine, 19(4), 736–744.

SIX
NATUROPATHY

Naturopathy, often regarded as a form of alternative medicine, emphasizes the body's intrinsic ability to heal itself. It integrates natural therapies such as herbal remedies, nutrition, exercise, and lifestyle modifications, often combined with non-invasive techniques.

Principles

Naturopathy is based on six key principles:

1. **The Healing Power of Nature**: The body has a natural ability to heal itself when supported correctly.
2. **Identify and Treat the Cause**: Focus on addressing root causes rather than just alleviating symptoms.
3. **First Do No Harm**: Use treatments that minimize harm and side effects.
4. **Treat the Whole Person**: Address physical, emotional, mental, and spiritual aspects.
5. **Doctor as Teacher**: Educate and empower patients to take charge of their health.
6. **Prevention**: Emphasize lifestyle choices and interventions that prevent disease.

Therapies Used in Naturopathy

- **Diet and Nutrition**: Personalized meal plans, detoxification diets, and supplementation.
- **Herbal Medicine**: Use of plants and plant extracts to treat ailments.
- **Physical Therapies**: Massage, acupuncture, hydrotherapy, and chiropractic adjustments.
- **Mind-Body Techniques**: Yoga, meditation, and stress management.
- **Lifestyle Counseling**: Guidance on exercise, sleep hygiene, and stress reduction.

Naturopathy as Alternative Medicine

- **Benefits**:

  - Focuses on preventive care.
  - Holistic approach often complements conventional treatments.
  - Fewer side effects when compared to pharmaceutical interventions.

- **Challenges**:

  - Lack of robust clinical trials for some treatments.
  - Perception as pseudoscience in some circles.
  - Potential risks of delaying conventional medical care for serious conditions.

Integration with Conventional Medicine

Many practitioners advocate for an integrative approach, combining naturopathy with evidence-based conventional medicine. For example, naturopathic remedies might be used to manage chronic conditions or alleviate side effects of traditional treatments.

Historical Background

Naturopathy dates back to ancient healing traditions, drawing influences from:

- **Traditional Medicine**: Ancient Egyptian, Chinese, and Indian systems of healing, such as Ayurveda and Traditional Chinese Medicine (TCM).
- **Hippocratic Philosophy**: The Greek physician Hippocrates emphasized natural healing, balanced diet, and lifestyle changes.
- **Modern Naturopathy**: Coined in the late 19th century by Dr. Benedict Lust, a German physician, naturopathy integrated European natural therapies with new scientific understanding.

Core Modalities in Naturopathy

Naturopathy combines various modalities under one practice. Some of the most prominent are:

1. Herbal Medicine

- **Description**: Use of plants and plant extracts for therapeutic purposes.
- **Examples**: Chamomile for anxiety, turmeric for inflammation, and echinacea for immune support.
- **Research**: Many herbs have documented benefits, but proper dosage and interactions need careful consideration.

2. Nutrition Therapy

- **Approach**: Focus on nutrient-rich, whole foods to support bodily functions.
- **Common Strategies**: Detox diets, elimination diets (e.g., for food sensitivities), and supplementation.
- **Evidence**: Strong backing for balanced diets and specific nutrients like omega-3s and antioxidants.

3. Physical Therapies

- **Hydrotherapy**: Use of water (e.g., baths, steam) to promote circulation and detoxification.
- **Massage Therapy**: Improves blood flow, reduces tension, and aids recovery.
- **Exercise and Movement**: Tailored regimens like yoga and Pilates to enhance flexibility, strength, and mental well-being.

4. Mind-Body Medicine

- **Stress Reduction**: Techniques like mindfulness meditation, deep breathing, and guided imagery.
- **Emotional Well-being**: Therapies address the impact of mental health on physical conditions.

5. Homeopathy (Sometimes Included)

- Involves diluted substances aimed at stimulating the body's self-healing responses. While controversial, some naturopaths include it in their practice.

Scientific Evidence and Criticism
Evidence Supporting Naturopathy

1. **Chronic Conditions**: Effective in managing lifestyle diseases like diabetes, hypertension, and obesity.
2. **Complementary Care**: Helps alleviate symptoms like fatigue, nausea, or stress during cancer treatment.
3. **Holistic Approach**: Recognized for fostering overall well-being and patient-centred care.

Criticism

1. **Limited Clinical Trials**: Some therapies lack large-scale, randomized controlled trials (RCTs).
2. **Regulation Variability**: Standards for training and certification differ across countries, leading to inconsistency.
3. **Risk of Misuse**: Delay or rejection of conventional medicine for critical illnesses can have serious consequences.

Integration with Conventional Medicine
Complementary Role

- **Functional Medicine**: Some physicians incorporate naturopathic principles, emphasizing root-cause analysis and patient education.
- **Hospitals and Clinics**: Many healthcare centers now offer integrative medicine programs blending naturopathy with evidence-based medical care.

Conditions Often Treated with Naturopathy

- **Chronic Conditions**: Arthritis, migraines, and digestive disorders.
- **Acute Ailments**: Colds, allergies, and infections.

- **Mental Health**: Stress, anxiety, and mild depression.

Regulation and Training
Education

- Naturopaths undergo rigorous training at accredited institutions, covering anatomy, physiology, biochemistry, and clinical practice.
- Some countries (e.g., the US, Canada, Australia) have licensed naturopathic doctors (NDs) with formalized education.

Certification and Standards

- Licensing laws vary globally, with some regions regulating naturopathy strictly and others offering minimal oversight.

The Future of Naturopathy

1. **Research Growth**: Increased focus on evidence-based studies.
2. **Integration**: More collaboration with conventional healthcare systems.
3. **Technological Advancements**: Use of AI and data analytics for personalized treatment plans.

Naturopathy techniques
1. Nutritional Techniques
Nutritional strategies play a foundational role in naturopathy.

- **Dietary Counseling**: Assessing and modifying a patient's diet to ensure proper nutrition.

  - Example: Anti-inflammatory diets for arthritis or a Mediterranean diet for heart health.

- **Supplementation**: Recommending vitamins, minerals, or herbs to address deficiencies.

  - Example: Vitamin D for bone health or probiotics for gut health.

- **Detoxification Diets**: Promoting liver and kidney detox through specific diets or fasting.

  - Example: Juice cleanses or elimination diets.

2. Herbal and Botanical Medicine

- **Herbal Infusions and Teas**: Preparing medicinal teas from plants like chamomile, ginger, or peppermint.
- **Tinctures**: Concentrated liquid extracts of herbs used for targeted effects.

  - Example: Echinacea tincture to support immune health.

- **Essential Oils**: Aromatherapy using oils like lavender for relaxation or eucalyptus for respiratory issues.

3. Physical Techniques
Hydrotherapy

- **Contrast Hydrotherapy**: Alternating hot and cold water to improve circulation and reduce inflammation.
- **Steam Baths and Saunas**: Used for detoxification and respiratory health.
- **Cold Compresses**: Relieve pain, swelling, or inflammation.

Massage Therapy

- Focused on relieving tension, improving circulation, and promoting relaxation.
- Techniques include Swedish massage, deep tissue massage, and lymphatic drainage.

Exercise Therapy

- **Yoga**: Combines physical postures, breathing exercises, and mindfulness.
- **Pilates**: Focuses on core strength, flexibility, and posture.
- **Rehabilitative Exercises**: Tailored routines for injury recovery or chronic pain.

4. Mind-Body Techniques
Meditation and Mindfulness

- Used to reduce stress, enhance focus, and improve mental clarity.
- Techniques include guided imagery, transcendental meditation, and progressive muscle relaxation.

Breathwork

- Exercises like diaphragmatic breathing or alternate nostril breathing to improve oxygenation and relaxation.

Biofeedback

- Using devices to monitor physiological responses and teach control over functions like heart rate and blood pressure.

5. Manual Therapies
Chiropractic Adjustments

- Focused on spinal alignment to alleviate pain and improve mobility.

Osteopathy

- Gentle manipulation of the musculoskeletal system to restore balance and function.

Acupressure

- Applying pressure to specific points on the body to relieve tension and improve energy flow.

6. Energy-Based Techniques

- **Reiki**: Hands-on or hands-off energy healing to promote balance and reduce stress.
- **Healing Touch**: Similar to Reiki but includes guided intentions to improve well-being.

- **Magnet Therapy**: Use of magnetic fields to improve blood flow and reduce pain.

7. Detoxification Techniques

- **Colon Hydrotherapy**: Cleansing the colon with water to improve digestion.
- **Dry Brushing**: Exfoliating the skin to stimulate lymphatic flow.
- **Chelation Therapy**: Removing heavy metals from the body using specific agents (requires careful supervision).

8. Homeopathy (Optional in Some Practices)

- Administering highly diluted substances to stimulate the body's self-healing mechanisms.

  - Example: Arnica for bruising or Nux vomica for digestive upset.

9. Lifestyle Counseling

- **Stress Management**: Strategies include time management, emotional awareness, and relaxation techniques.
- **Sleep Hygiene**: Guidance on improving sleep quality through environment optimization and routines.
- **Behavioral Changes**: Encouraging habits like regular exercise, hydration, and avoiding toxins like alcohol and tobacco.

10. Diagnostic Techniques

- **Iridology**: Examining the iris of the eye to detect underlying health conditions.
- **Kinesiology**: Assessing muscle strength and movement patterns.
- **Pulse and Tongue Diagnosis**: Borrowed from Traditional Chinese Medicine and Ayurveda.

Combination Techniques

Many naturopaths use a combination of the above methods tailored to individual needs, creating a personalized treatment plan.

Conclusion

Naturopathy provides a holistic framework for health and wellness, emphasizing natural and preventive care. While it offers valuable approaches, its effectiveness varies, and patients are encouraged to consult qualified professionals and consider evidence-based practices when choosing treatment options.

BIBLIOGARPHY

- Sarris, J., & Wardle, J. (2010). Clinical naturopathy: An evidence-based guide to practice. Complementary Therapies in Medicine, 18(2), 56–62.
- Pizzorno, J. E., & Murray, M. T. (2012). Textbook of natural medicine (4th ed.). Elsevier Health Sciences.
- Wardle, J., Adams, J., Lui, C. W., & Steel, A. (2013). Current challenges and future directions for naturopathic medicine. Journal of Alternative and Complementary Medicine, 19(1), 12–14.
- Posadzki, P., Watson, L., & Ernst, E. (2013). Complementary and alternative medicine (CAM) therapies in the management of pain: A systematic

review. Rheumatology International, 33(6), 1543–1560.

- Ernst, E. (2011). The role of complementary and alternative medicine. British Medical Journal, 342, d3712.
- Bradley, R., Harnett, J., Cooley, K., McIntyre, E., & Adams, J. (2020). Naturopathy as a model of prevention-oriented, patient-centered care: Evidence and challenges. Journal of Alternative and Complementary Medicine, 26(5), 429–432.
- Barnes, J., Anderson, L. A., & Phillipson, J. D. (2007). Herbal medicines (3rd ed.). Pharmaceutical Press.
- Kovacs, F. M., et al. (2008). The effectiveness of hydrotherapy in the treatment of low back pain: A systematic review. Journal of Back and Musculoskeletal Rehabilitation, 21(3), 111–120.
- Goyal, M., Singh, S., Sibinga, E. M. S., et al. (2014). Meditation programs for psychological stress and well-being: A systematic review and meta-analysis. JAMA Internal Medicine, 174(3), 357–368.

SEVEN
AROMATHERAPY

Aromatherapy, a holistic healing treatment that uses natural plant extracts to promote health and well-being, is increasingly recognized as a form of alternative medicine. Essential oils, extracted from flowers, leaves, stems, bark, and roots, are at the core of aromatherapy practices.

Aromatherapy involves the use of aromatic essential oils to improve physical, emotional, and psychological health. The practice dates back thousands of years to ancient cultures, including Egyptian, Chinese, and Indian traditions, where aromatic plants were used for religious, therapeutic, and cosmetic purposes.

Historical Background

Aromatherapy has deep historical roots:

- **Ancient Egypt**: Essential oils were used for embalming, cosmetics, and religious rituals.
- **China and India**: Aromatic plants played a role in traditional medicine like Ayurveda and acupuncture.
- **Greece and Rome**: Physicians such as Hippocrates used aromatic oils for massage and healing purposes.

- **Modern Revival**: The term "aromatherapy" was coined by French chemist René-Maurice Gattefossé in the 20th century after he discovered the healing properties of lavender oil.

Key Techniques in Aromatherapy

1. **Inhalation**:

   - Through diffusers, sprays, or steam.
   - Benefits: Quick absorption via the nasal passages, affecting the limbic system directly.

2. **Massage**:

   - Essential oils are diluted in carrier oils (e.g., almond, coconut, or jojoba) and applied to the skin.
   - Benefits: Combines the therapeutic effects of massage with the benefits of essential oils.

3. **Baths**:

   - Oils are added to warm baths, creating a relaxing and therapeutic environment.
   - Benefits: Absorbed through both inhalation and the skin.

4. **Compresses**:

   - A cloth soaked in water mixed with essential oils is applied to specific areas of the body.
   - Benefits: Useful for localized pain or inflammation.

5. **Direct Application** (with caution):

   - Certain oils like tea tree or lavender can sometimes be applied directly to the skin for wounds or acne.

Advantages of Aromatherapy as Alternative Medicine

- **Non-Invasive**: It is a gentle and natural approach to healing.
- **Complementary**: Can be used alongside conventional medicine.
- **Personalized**: Tailored blends and methods cater to individual needs.

Common Essential Oils and Their Uses

- **Lavender**: Relaxation, sleep aid, anxiety reduction.
- **Peppermint**: Energy boost, headache relief, digestive aid
- **Eucalyptus**: Decongestant, anti-inflammatory
- **Tea Tree**: Antimicrobial, acne treatment, wound healing
- **Lemon**: Mood enhancement, immune system support
- **Chamomile**: Calming, anti-inflammatory, skin-soothing
- **Rosemary**: Mental clarity, improved memory, hair health

Mechanisms of Action

Aromatherapy works through two primary mechanisms:

1. **Olfactory Pathway**:

   - Scent molecules stimulate olfactory nerves, sending signals to the limbic system, which governs emotions

and memory.
- This can reduce stress hormones like cortisol and enhance mood.

2. **Topical Absorption**:

- Active compounds in essential oils penetrate the skin and enter the bloodstream.
- For example, menthol in peppermint can relax muscles and reduce inflammation.

Scientific Studies and Evidence

- **Stress and Anxiety**:
Studies show that lavender essential oil can reduce anxiety in clinical settings, including pre-operative patients.
- **Pain Relief**:
A 2015 study found that peppermint oil significantly reduced tension headaches compared to a placebo.
- **Sleep Disorders**:
Aromatherapy with lavender has been shown to improve sleep quality in insomniacs and the elderly.
- **Immune Function**:
Eucalyptus and tea tree oils possess antimicrobial properties, making them effective against certain infections.

Advantages of Aromatherapy

- **Customizable**: Blends can be tailored to individual preferences and needs.

- **Accessible**: Many essential oils are widely available and affordable.
- **Few Side Effects**: When used properly, the risks are minimal compared to pharmaceutical drugs.

Safety and Risks

While generally safe, there are precautions to take:

- **Dilution**: Essential oils are potent and must be diluted in a carrier oil to prevent skin irritation.
- **Patch Testing**: Before applying a new oil, perform a patch test to rule out allergies.
- **Pregnancy and Children**: Certain oils (e.g., rosemary, clary sage) are contraindicated during pregnancy or for young children.
- **Photosensitivity**: Citrus oils can cause skin reactions when exposed to sunlight.

Integrating Aromatherapy in Modern Medicine

Aromatherapy is increasingly being integrated into healthcare:

- **Hospitals**: Used in palliative care to reduce pain, anxiety, and improve quality of life.
- **Mental Health**: Complementary therapy for depression and anxiety disorders.
- **Rehabilitation**: Helps in physical therapy for muscle relaxation and pain management.

Limitations

1. **Lack of Regulation**: The essential oil industry lacks stringent quality control, leading to potential

contamination or adulteration.

2. **Placebo Effect**: Some benefits may stem from psychological rather than physiological effects.
3. **Not a Cure-All**: Aromatherapy is complementary and should not replace conventional medical treatments for serious conditions.
4. Contraindications: Certain oils may not be safe for pregnant women, children, or individuals with specific medical conditions.

Conclusion and Future Directions

Aromatherapy bridges ancient practices and modern wellness trends, offering a natural, non-invasive approach to health. While promising, it's most effective when used as part of a comprehensive health plan, guided by evidence and professional advice. Aromatherapy as an alternative medicine offers a natural, holistic approach to health and wellness. While it holds promise for addressing certain conditions, it is best used as a complementary therapy rather than a standalone treatment. Consulting a qualified practitioner and ensuring the use of high-quality essential oils are essential for safe and effective practice.

BIBLIOGARPHY

- Buchbauer, G. (2010). "Biological activities of essential oils and their fragrance compounds." Natural Product Communications, 5(8), 1365-1372.
- Ali, B., Al-Wabel, N. A., Shams, S., et al. (2015). "Essential oils used in aromatherapy: A systemic review." Asian Pacific Journal of Tropical Biomedicine, 5(8), 601-611.
- Perry, N., & Perry, E. (2006). "Aromatherapy in the management of psychiatric disorders." CNS Drugs, 20(4),

257-280.

- Zhang, J., Yang, L., et al. (2017). "Chemical compositions and bioactivities of essential oils from seven Citrus species." Molecules, 22(8), 1290.
- Lee, Y. L., & Lee, H. J. (2006). "Effects of lavender aromatherapy on insomnia and depression in women college students." Journal of Korean Academy of Nursing, 36(1), 136-143.
- Goel, N., Kim, H., & Lao, R. P. (2005). "An olfactory stimulus modifies nighttime sleep in young men and women." Chronobiology International, 22(5), 889-904.
- Lillehei, A. S., & Halcon, L. L. (2014). "A systematic review of the effect of inhaled essential oils on sleep." Journal of Alternative and Complementary Medicine, 20(6), 441-451.
- Ali, B., Al-Wabel, N. A., et al. (2015). "Essential oils used in aromatherapy: A systemic review." Asian Pacific Journal of Tropical Biomedicine, 5(8), 601-611.
- Herz, R. S. (2009). "Aromatherapy facts and fictions: A scientific analysis of olfactory effects on mood, physiology, and behavior." International Journal of Neuroscience, 119(2), 263-290.
- Tisserand, R., & Young, R. (2013). Essential Oil Safety: A Guide for Health Care Professionals. Churchill Livingstone.
- Posadzki, P., Alotaibi, A., & Ernst, E. (2012). "Adverse effects of aromatherapy: A systematic review of case reports and case series." International Journal of Risk & Safety in Medicine, 24(3), 147-161.
- Lin, P. C., et al. (2019). "Aromatherapy as an intervention for improving mental health outcomes in older adults: A systematic review and meta-analysis of randomized controlled trials." Journal of Clinical Nursing, 28(23-24),

4369-4384.

- Zhang, Z. J., et al. (2021). "Aromatherapy in treating stress: Mechanisms and clinical applications." Frontiers in Psychology, 12, 620897.

EIGHT
YOGA

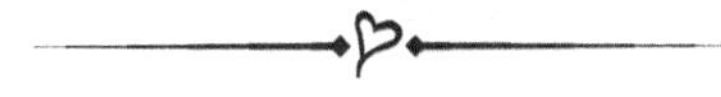

Yoga, an ancient practice originating in India, is widely recognized as a complementary and alternative medicine (CAM) approach. It integrates physical postures (asanas), breath control (pranayama), meditation, and ethical principles to promote holistic well-being. Yoga has gained popularity in healthcare for managing chronic conditions, enhancing mental health, and improving overall quality of life.

Principles of Yoga

1. **Union of Mind, Body, and Spirit**: Yoga emphasizes harmony between physical, mental, and spiritual dimensions.
2. **Holistic Healing**: Focuses on prevention, healing, and achieving balance.
3. **Self-Awareness**: Encourages mindfulness and awareness of bodily sensations and emotions.

Therapeutic Applications of Yoga
Yoga has been integrated into medical and therapeutic contexts to address various physical and psychological

conditions:

1. Stress Management

- Practices: Meditation, deep breathing, and relaxation techniques.
- Benefits: Reduces cortisol levels, lowers blood pressure, and improves resilience to stress.
- Example Poses: Child's Pose (Balasana), Legs-Up-The-Wall Pose (Viparita Karani).

2. Pain Management

- Conditions: Chronic low back pain, arthritis, migraines.
- Mechanism: Improves flexibility, strengthens muscles, and reduces inflammation.
- Example Poses: Cat-Cow Stretch (Marjaryasana-Bitilasana), Bridge Pose (Setu Bandhasana).

3. Cardiovascular Health

- Benefits: Enhances heart rate variability, reduces hypertension, and improves circulation.
- Example Poses: Mountain Pose (Tadasana), Tree Pose (Vrikshasana).

4. Mental Health

- Conditions: Anxiety, depression, PTSD, and insomnia.
- Mechanism: Activates the parasympathetic nervous system, enhances serotonin levels.
- Practices: Alternate nostril breathing (Nadi Shodhana), Corpse Pose (Savasana).

5. Respiratory Disorders

- Conditions: Asthma, COPD, and sinusitis.
- Benefits: Strengthens respiratory muscles and improves lung capacity.
- Practices: Kapalabhati (cleansing breath), Ujjayi (ocean breath).

6. Metabolic and Endocrine Disorders

- Conditions: Diabetes, thyroid imbalance, and obesity.
- Benefits: Stimulates endocrine glands, regulates metabolism.
- Example Poses: Bow Pose (Dhanurasana), Shoulder Stand (Sarvangasana).

7. Neurological Conditions

- Conditions: Stroke recovery, multiple sclerosis, and Parkinson's disease.
- Benefits: Enhances coordination, balance, and neuroplasticity.
- Example Poses: Warrior II (Virabhadrasana II), Seated Forward Bend (Paschimottanasana).

Evidence Supporting Yoga as Medicine

- **Pain Management**: Yoga has been shown to reduce chronic pain through improved posture and musculoskeletal alignment.
- **Mental Health**: Studies highlight yoga's role in reducing symptoms of anxiety and depression.

- **Cardiovascular Benefits**: Research suggests regular yoga practice lowers blood pressure and cholesterol.
- **Diabetes Management**: Yoga improves glycemic control and reduces stress in type 2 diabetes patients.

Yoga Techniques and Components

1. **Asanas (Physical Postures)**:

   - Improve flexibility, strength, and posture.
   - Examples: Downward Dog, Cobra Pose.

2. **Pranayama (Breathing Techniques)**:

   - Enhance respiratory efficiency and mental clarity.
   - Examples: Anulom Vilom, Bhastrika.

3. **Meditation**:

   - Promotes relaxation and mindfulness.
   - Examples: Mindfulness meditation, mantra meditation.

4. **Shatkarmas (Cleansing Techniques)**:

   - Detoxify the body.
   - Examples: Neti (nasal cleansing), Dhauti (stomach cleansing).

5. **Relaxation Techniques**:

   - Reduce physical and mental tension.
   - Example: Yoga Nidra (Yogic Sleep).

Integration in Healthcare

- **Yoga Therapy**: Tailored practices based on individual health conditions.
- **Complementary Approach**: Used alongside conventional treatments for holistic care.
- **Workplace Wellness**: Yoga programs for reducing workplace stress and enhancing productivity.

Limitations and Considerations

1. **Safety**: Certain poses may not be suitable for individuals with specific medical conditions.
2. **Qualified Guidance**: Should be practiced under a trained instructor, especially for therapeutic purposes.
3. **Consistency**: Benefits require regular and long-term practice.
4. **Individualization**: Practices should be customized to meet personal health needs.

Conclusion

Yoga is a versatile and accessible form of alternative medicine that complements modern healthcare. Its integration into physiotherapy, mental health programs, and chronic disease management highlights its potential to enhance overall well-being. When practiced safely and consistently, yoga offers a sustainable path to physical and emotional health.

BIBLIOGRAPHY

- Goyal, M., et al. (2014). Meditation programs for psychological stress and well-being: a systematic review and meta-analysis. JAMA Internal Medicine, 174(3), 357-368.

- Saper, R. B., et al. (2017). Yoga, physical therapy, or education for chronic low back pain: a randomized noninferiority trial. Annals of Internal Medicine, 167(2), 85-94.
- Cramer, H., et al. (2014). Yoga for cardiovascular events: a systematic review. European Journal of Preventive Cardiology, 21(1), 76-85.
- Streeter, C. C., et al. (2010). Effects of yoga versus walking on mood, anxiety, and brain GABA levels: a randomized controlled MRS study. The Journal of Alternative and Complementary Medicine, 16(11), 1145-1152.
- Gupta, S. K., et al. (2016). Effect of yoga based lifestyle intervention on state and trait anxiety. Indian Journal of Physiology and Pharmacology, 60(4), 407-414.
- Kumar, K., et al. (2018). Effectiveness of yoga as a therapeutic intervention in the management of type 2 diabetes mellitus. The International Journal of Yoga, 11(2), 183-189.
- Satyananda, S. (2007). Yoga Nidra: A Yogic Sleep for Modern Times. Yoga Publications Trust.
- Brown, R. P., & Gerbarg, P. L. (2005). Sudarshan Kriya yogic breathing in the treatment of stress, anxiety, and depression: part II—clinical applications and guidelines. The Journal of Alternative and Complementary Medicine, 11(4), 711-717.
- Khalsa, S. B. S., et al. (2015). Yoga as a therapeutic intervention for major depressive disorder: a meta-analysis of randomized controlled trials. Frontiers in Psychiatry, 6, 195.
- Saraswati, S. S. (2002). Asana Pranayama Mudra Bandha. Yoga Publications Trust.

- Rani, K. R., et al. (2011). Effects of yoga nidra on sleep in patients with chronic insomnia: a randomized clinical trial. Indian Journal of Psychiatry, 53(2), 172-176.
- Field, T. (2016). Yoga research review. Complementary Therapies in Clinical Practice, 24, 145-161.
- World Health Organization. (2002). Traditional Medicine Strategy 2002–2005.

NINE

CUPPING THERAPY

Cupping therapy is an alternative therapy that has been practiced for centuries in various cultures, including traditional Chinese medicine, Middle Eastern medicine, and other healing traditions. It involves the use of cups, typically made of glass, bamboo, silicone, or plastic, that are placed on the skin to create suction. This suction is believed to help improve circulation, relieve muscle tension, and promote healing.

Types of Cupping Therapy:

1. **Dry Cupping**: Involves the application of cups to the skin without making any incisions.
2. **Wet Cupping**: Includes a small incision in the skin before applying the cup, allowing a small amount of blood to be drawn.
3. **Fire Cupping**: Uses heat to create the suction inside the cup, often by briefly heating the air inside before placing it on the skin.

4. **Silicone Cupping**: Uses flexible silicone cups that can glide over the skin for a massage-like effect.

Claimed Benefits:

- **Pain Relief**: May alleviate muscle pain, back pain, and tension.
- **Improved Circulation**: Stimulates blood flow in the treated area.
- **Detoxification**: Some proponents claim it helps remove toxins from the body.
- **Stress Reduction**: Relaxing and soothing effects may reduce stress and anxiety.
- **Skin Health**: May improve skin conditions like acne or eczema.
- **Respiratory Relief**: Used to treat colds, asthma, and other respiratory issues in traditional medicine.

How It Works:

The suction from the cups pulls the skin and underlying tissues upward, which is thought to stimulate blood flow and promote the healing of soft tissues. In wet cupping, the slight bleeding may be intended to remove what practitioners describe as "stagnant" blood or toxins.

Scientific Evidence:

- The evidence supporting cupping therapy is mixed. Some studies suggest it may be effective for certain conditions, such as chronic pain, but the overall quality of research is low.
- The placebo effect might also contribute to its perceived benefits.

Risks and Precautions:

- Bruising, skin irritation, or burns are common side effects.
- Wet cupping carries a risk of infection if not performed under sterile conditions.
- It is not recommended for individuals with bleeding disorders, skin conditions, or those who are pregnant.

Historical and Cultural Context of Cupping Therapy:
Cupping therapy has deep roots in various traditional healing systems, with evidence of its use dating back thousands of years. It is mentioned in ancient Egyptian, Chinese, and Middle Eastern medical texts. For instance:

- **Ancient Egypt**: The Ebers Papyrus (1550 BCE) describes the use of cupping therapy for treating various ailments.
- **Traditional Chinese Medicine (TCM)**: Cupping is an integral part of TCM, often combined with acupuncture. It is used to balance the flow of qi (energy) and remove blockages in the meridians.
- **Islamic Medicine**: Known as *hijama*, cupping therapy is mentioned in Hadith (sayings of the Prophet Muhammad) as a recommended treatment.

Modern Applications and Uses:
Cupping therapy has gained popularity in modern wellness and sports recovery settings. Athletes, in particular, have embraced it as part of their recovery regimen. For example, prominent Olympians and professional athletes have been seen with the telltale circular marks of cupping therapy.

Common Applications:

1. **Sports Recovery**: Reduces muscle soreness and enhances recovery after intense physical activity.
2. **Chronic Pain Management**: Used for conditions like arthritis, fibromyalgia, and lower back pain.
3. **Migraine Relief**: Some individuals report fewer migraines after undergoing cupping therapy.
4. **Digestive Health**: Believed to aid in alleviating symptoms of IBS or constipation.
5. **Immune System Boosting**: Used in traditional practices to support immune function, especially during seasonal changes.

Techniques and Equipment:

Cupping therapy has evolved, with modern adaptations enhancing its versatility:

1. **Vacuum Cupping**: Uses a pump to create suction, replacing the traditional fire method for a safer and more controlled process.
2. **Massage Cupping**: Cups are moved across oiled skin, combining the benefits of cupping with massage.
3. **Facial Cupping**: Smaller, gentler cups are used on the face to improve circulation and reduce puffiness.

Research and Scientific Perspective:

While cupping therapy has been widely studied, the scientific community remains divided on its effectiveness. Some highlights from research include:

1. **Pain Relief**: Systematic reviews suggest cupping therapy may reduce chronic neck and back pain, potentially through improved blood flow and reduced muscle tightness.

2. **Inflammation**: Some studies indicate cupping might reduce markers of inflammation, though the mechanisms are not fully understood.
3. **Psychological Benefits**: Anecdotal evidence suggests relaxation effects that could help with anxiety and stress.

Popularity in Complementary Medicine

Cupping therapy is often combined with other alternative treatments such as:

- **Acupuncture**: Enhances therapeutic effects by targeting specific acupoints.
- **Herbal Medicine**: Paired with herbal remedies in traditional practices.
- **Yoga and Meditation**: Used alongside mindfulness practices for holistic healing.

Safety Guidelines and Best Practices

For those considering cupping therapy, it's essential to follow these precautions:

- **Choose a Qualified Practitioner**: Ensure the therapist is certified and uses sterile equipment.
- **Discuss Health History**: Share any medical conditions, medications, or allergies with the therapist.
- **Observe Aftercare**: Avoid hot baths or exposure to cold air on the treated area to prevent irritation.
- **Monitor Skin Reaction**: Bruising is common, but if you experience severe pain, blistering, or infection, consult a doctor.

Criticisms and Challenges:

1. **Lack of Standardization**: Techniques, materials, and durations vary widely.
2. **Placebo Effect**: Critics argue that some of the benefits might be psychological rather than physiological.
3. **Overuse of "Detox" Claims**: Scientific evidence for detoxification through cupping remains sparse.

Final Thoughts

Cupping therapy bridges the gap between ancient wisdom and modern wellness trends. While it may not be a panacea, it can be a valuable tool for certain conditions when used responsibly. Research is ongoing, and its integration into evidence-based practices could enhance its credibility and application. As with any alternative therapy, an individualized approach and open communication with healthcare providers are key to achieving the best outcomes.

Conclusion:

Cupping therapy may offer relief for some conditions and is often used as a complementary treatment alongside conventional medicine. However, it should be approached with caution, and individuals should consult with a healthcare provider before starting cupping therapy to ensure it is safe and appropriate for their specific health needs.

BIBLIOGRAPHY

- Ghalioungui, P. (1963). *The Ebers Papyrus: A New English Translation.* Academy of Scientific Research and Technology.
- Wang, J., & Liang, B. (2006). *Cupping therapy: A modern practitioner's guide to ancient Chinese medicine.* Churchill

Livingstone.

- Rahman, S., & Zainudin, M. F. (2017). "Cupping therapy (Hijama): A review of the evidence." *The Middle East Journal of Family Medicine*, 15(10), 30-35.
- Markovic, M., et al. (2020). "Effects of dry cupping therapy on recovery after physical activity." *Journal of Sports Science & Medicine*, 19(2), 332-341.
- Kim, J., & Lee, M. S. (2011). "Cupping for treating pain: A systematic review." *The Journal of Alternative and Complementary Medicine*, 17(10), 781-787.
- Farhadi, K., et al. (2009). "The effectiveness of wet-cupping in the treatment of tension and migraine headache." *American Journal of Chinese Medicine*, 37(1), 113-120.
- Cao, H., et al. (2012). "Cupping therapy for chronic pain: A systematic review and meta-analysis." *PLoS One*, 7(2), e31793.
- Tagil, S. M., et al. (2014). "Wet cupping therapy improves health-related quality of life in patients with fibromyalgia: A randomized controlled trial." *The Journal of Pain*, 15(4), 355-364.
- Lao, L., et al. (2015). "Complementary therapies for stress management: A systematic review." *Journal of Integrative Medicine*, 13(3), 130-140.
- El Sayed, S. M., et al. (2013). "Methods of wet cupping therapy (Al-hijamah): In light of modern medicine and prophetic medicine." *Alternative and Integrative Medicine*, 2(5), 1-16.
- Ernst, E. (2009). "Cupping therapy: An overview of systematic reviews." *Journal of Postgraduate Medicine*, 55(3), 194-199.
- Bent, S. (2008). "Herbal medicine in the United States: Review of efficacy, safety, and regulation." *Journal of*

General Internal Medicine, 23(6), 854-859.

• 71 •

TEN
TAI CHI

Tai Chi is an ancient Chinese martial art that has evolved into a popular form of exercise and alternative therapy known for its gentle, flowing movements and emphasis on mindfulness. It combines physical activity, relaxation, and meditation, making it a holistic practice with numerous potential health benefits.

Benefits of Tai Chi as an Alternative Therapy
Physical Health:

- *Improved Balance and Coordination:* Tai Chi enhances proprioception and strengthens muscles, which can reduce the risk of falls, particularly in older adults.
- *Joint Health:* The low-impact movements are beneficial for individuals with arthritis or joint pain, as they promote flexibility without stressing the joints.
- *Cardiovascular Benefits:* Regular practice may improve heart health by enhancing circulation and reducing blood pressure.

Mental Health:

- *Stress Reduction:* The meditative aspects of Tai Chi help calm the mind, reduce cortisol levels, and improve emotional well-being.
- *Enhanced Focus and Cognitive Function:* Studies suggest that Tai Chi can improve attention, memory, and overall cognitive abilities, particularly in older adults.
- *Anxiety and Depression:* The rhythmic, mindful movements can alleviate symptoms of anxiety and mild to moderate depression.

Chronic Conditions:

- *Pain Management:* Tai Chi has been shown to reduce chronic pain, including conditions like fibromyalgia and lower back pain.
- *Improved Quality of Life:* It supports overall well-being for individuals managing conditions such as Parkinson's disease, multiple sclerosis, and cancer.
- *Boosted Immune Function:* Regular practice may enhance the immune system and improve the body's resilience to illness.

Rehabilitation:

- *Post-Surgery Recovery:* Tai Chi can aid in recovery by improving mobility and reducing post-operative complications.
- *Stroke Rehabilitation:* It may help regain motor skills and improve balance in stroke survivors.

Origins and Philosophy of Tai Chi
Tai Chi, also known as Tai Chi Chuan, originated as a martial art in ancient China and is deeply rooted in Taoist

philosophy. It emphasizes harmony, balance, and the flow of energy, often referred to as "Qi" or "Chi." Practitioners focus on slow, deliberate movements that align body, mind, and spirit, reflecting the Taoist principle of balance, such as the interplay of yin and yang.

Expanded Benefits of Tai Chi

1. Physical Health

- *Muscle Strength and Endurance:* Tai Chi strengthens core muscles, improves endurance, and enhances physical stability.
- *Bone Health:* Regular practice has shown potential in slowing the progression of bone density loss in individuals with osteoporosis.
- *Improved Posture:* The practice encourages body awareness and alignment, which can help alleviate postural issues.

2. Mental and Emotional Health

- *Mindfulness and Emotional Regulation:* Tai Chi integrates mindfulness techniques, helping individuals manage emotional challenges and improve resilience.
- *Sleep Improvement:* Studies suggest Tai Chi may improve sleep quality in individuals with insomnia or disrupted sleep patterns.
- *Social Interaction:* Group Tai Chi classes foster a sense of community and reduce feelings of isolation, particularly in older adults.

3. Support for Chronic Conditions

- *Diabetes Management:* Research indicates that Tai Chi can help regulate blood sugar levels and improve metabolic function in individuals with type 2 diabetes.
- *Respiratory Health:* The deep breathing techniques of Tai Chi can benefit individuals with asthma or chronic obstructive pulmonary disease (COPD).
- *Cancer Recovery:* Many cancer survivors use Tai Chi to manage fatigue, improve physical function, and enhance emotional well-being during or after treatment.

4. Neurological Benefits

- *Parkinson's Disease*: Tai Chi has been shown to improve balance, motor control, and quality of life for individuals with Parkinson's.
- *Stroke Recovery:* It supports neuromuscular coordination and confidence in movement during rehabilitation.
- *Cognitive Decline:* Preliminary studies suggest Tai Chi may delay the onset of cognitive decline in individuals at risk of dementia.

Tai Chi Styles and Their Focus

There are several styles of Tai Chi, each emphasizing slightly different aspects:

- **Chen Style:** Combines slow and fast movements with bursts of power.
- **Yang Style:** The most widely practiced, featuring slow, gentle, and continuous movements.
- **Wu Style:** Focuses on smaller, more compact movements and subtle shifts in weight.
- **Sun Style:** Incorporates elements of Tai Chi, Qigong, and martial arts, often preferred for arthritis and mobility

issues.

- **Hao Style:** A lesser-known style, emphasizing precision and internal energy.

Conclusion

By addressing the physical, mental, and spiritual dimensions of health, Tai Chi stands out as a versatile and holistic therapy with the potential to improve quality of life for individuals across all age groups and health conditions.

BIBLIOGRAPHY

- Jahnke, R., Larkey, L., Rogers, C., Etnier, J., & Lin, F. (2010). A comprehensive review of health benefits of Qigong and Tai Chi. *American Journal of Health Promotion*, 24(6), e1-e25.
- Wayne, P. M., & Kaptchuk, T. J. (2008). Challenges inherent to Tai Chi research: Part I—Tai Chi as a complex multicomponent intervention. *The Journal of Alternative and Complementary Medicine*, 14(1), 95-102.
- Wang, C., Bannuru, R., Ramel, J., Kupelnick, B., Scott, T., & Schmid, C. H. (2010). Tai Chi on psychological well-being: Systematic review and meta-analysis. *BMC Complementary and Alternative Medicine*, 10(1), 23.
- Lavretsky, H., & Irwin, M. R. (2007). Tai Chi: A mind-body exercise in older adults. *Nature Reviews Rheumatology*, 3(4), 228-234.
- Yeh, G. Y., Wang, C., Wayne, P. M., & Phillips, R. S. (2008). Tai Chi exercise for patients with cardiovascular conditions and risk factors: A systematic review. *Journal of Cardiopulmonary Rehabilitation and Prevention*, 28(2), 85-96.

- Lee, M. S., Pittler, M. H., & Ernst, E. (2007). Tai Chi for rheumatoid arthritis: Systematic review. *Rheumatology (Oxford)*, 46(11), 1648-1651.
- Li, F., Harmer, P., Fitzgerald, K., Eckstrom, E., Stock, R., Galver, J., Maddalozzo, G., & Batya, S. S. (2012). Tai Chi and postural stability in patients with Parkinson's disease. *The New England Journal of Medicine*, 366(6), 511-519.
- Taylor-Piliae, R. E., & Coull, B. M. (2012). Community-based Tai Chi is associated with improved psychosocial well-being and reduced depressive symptoms in older stroke survivors. *American Journal of Geriatric Psychiatry*, 20(6), 548-556.
- Luo, J., Xu, H., Liu, X., & Zhang, M. (2017). Effects of Tai Chi on type 2 diabetes mellitus: A meta-analysis. *Journal of Diabetes Research*, 2017, Article ID 9241423.
- Rogers, C. E., Larkey, L. K., & Keller, C. (2009). A review of clinical trials of Tai Chi and Qigong in older adults. *Western Journal of Nursing Research*, 31(2), 245-279.
- Wayne, P. M., & Fuerst, M. L. (2013). *The Harvard Medical School Guide to Tai Chi: 12 Weeks to a Healthy Body, Strong Heart, and Sharp Mind*. Shambhala Publications.
- Yeh, G. Y., Chan, C. W., Wayne, P. M., & Conboy, L. (2016). The impact of Tai Chi exercise on self-efficacy, quality of life, and physical function in patients with chronic diseases. *Preventive Medicine Reports*, 2, 118-122.

ELEVEN
ZONING

Zoning as an alternative medicine practice refers to methods that align with principles of reflexology or energy medicine, where specific areas of the body, often called "zones," are believed to correspond to internal organs or systems. Practitioners claim that by manipulating or applying pressure to these zones, they can influence the body's overall health, balance energy, and address ailments.

Core Concepts of Zoning in Alternative Medicine

· **Zone Therapy:**

The body is divided into vertical or horizontal zones.
Reflex points, typically on the hands, feet, or face, correspond to organs or areas within these zones.
Stimulating these points is thought to promote healing and balance.

· **Energy Pathways:**

Zoning often involves the idea of energy flow (similar to concepts in acupuncture or Reiki).

Blockages in specific zones are believed to lead to physical or emotional ailments.

· **Tools and Techniques:**

Practitioners may use their hands, massage tools, or even subtle energy techniques.

Techniques can include pressing, rubbing, or stretching certain areas.

· **Holistic Approach:**

Zoning integrates physical, mental, and emotional health, aiming to treat the person as a whole rather than focusing solely on symptoms.

Applications

Stress Relief: Zoning is often used to reduce tension and promote relaxation.

Pain Management: It's said to help with chronic pain by addressing imbalances in specific zones.

Digestive and Hormonal Health: Some claim zoning can regulate internal organ function.

Emotional Well-being: Zoning is also used to address emotional or mental health issues.

Criticism and Evidence

Scientific Validation: Zoning lacks substantial scientific backing and is often criticized as pseudoscience. Most benefits reported by users are attributed to the placebo effect or general relaxation.

Regulation and Training: There are no universally recognized standards for zoning practitioners, so quality can vary.

Historical Origins of Zoning in Alternative Medicine

Zoning as a concept may draw inspiration from ancient healing traditions, though its specific use as an alternative medical practice evolved in the 20th century. Here's a deeper dive into its potential roots and evolution:

Ancient Healing Practices:

Chinese Medicine: Traditional Chinese Medicine (TCM) emphasizes energy flow through meridians, similar to the "zones" in zoning. Practices like acupuncture and acupressure align closely with zoning principles.

Ayurveda: The Indian system of Ayurveda discusses chakras (energy centers) and nadis (channels), which resonate with zoning's emphasis on energy balance.

Egyptian Reflexology: Ancient Egyptian texts and artifacts suggest the use of foot and hand mapping for therapeutic purposes.

Modern Developments:

William Fitzgerald (1872–1942): Often considered the father of modern zone therapy, Fitzgerald proposed dividing the body into 10 vertical zones. His work laid the foundation for reflexology and zoning practices.

Eunice Ingham (1889–1974): A physiotherapist who expanded on Fitzgerald's ideas, creating detailed maps of reflex points on the feet and hands. Zoning practitioners may still reference these maps.

Integration with Energy Medicine:

In the late 20th and early 21st centuries, zoning began incorporating elements of energy healing (e.g., Reiki, biofield therapies). This integration reflects a growing trend in alternative medicine to blend physical manipulation with spiritual or energetic principles.

How Zoning Works (Theoretically)

1. Mapping the Zones:

The body is divided into vertical or horizontal sections.

Each section corresponds to a specific internal organ or physiological function.

Reflex points within these zones (e.g., on the feet, hands, or face) act as access points for therapeutic intervention.

2. Stimulating Zones:

Physical Stimulation: Practitioners apply pressure, massage, or tapping techniques to stimulate specific zones.

Energy Healing: Some methods involve channeling or balancing subtle energy flows, requiring minimal physical contact.

Tools and Aids: Wooden sticks, rollers, or even essential oils might be used to enhance stimulation.

3. Holistic Effects:

Body: Improved circulation, reduced inflammation, and enhanced detoxification are common claims.

Mind: Stress reduction, emotional balance, and mental clarity are emphasized.

Spirit: Zoning is sometimes linked to spiritual growth, with claims of improving overall life force energy.

Benefits and Potential Uses

Stress and Anxiety Management:

- Helps calm the nervous system.
- Promotes deep relaxation, which may reduce cortisol levels.

Pain Relief:

- Commonly used for headaches, back pain, and joint issues.
- May help with chronic pain by improving local circulation and releasing muscle tension.

Improved Organ Function:

- Some practitioners claim zoning can enhance liver, kidney, or digestive health by stimulating related zones.

Hormonal Balance:

- Linked to claims of regulating menstrual cycles, alleviating menopausal symptoms, and supporting thyroid function.

Detoxification:

- Some believe zoning can stimulate the lymphatic system, aiding in the elimination of toxins.

Criticisms and Challenges

Lack of Scientific Evidence:

Zoning is often criticized for lacking rigorous scientific validation. Existing studies on reflexology and related practices suggest potential benefits, but results are inconsistent.

Placebo Effect:

Many benefits attributed to zoning may result from the placebo effect or general relaxation rather than specific physiological changes.

Standardization Issues:

No universal standards for zoning techniques, zones, or qualifications. This lack of regulation can lead to variability in practitioner quality and outcomes.

Safety Concerns:

Generally considered safe, but improper techniques might cause discomfort. Should not replace medical treatment for serious conditions.

BIBLIOGRAPHY

- Fitzgerald, W. H. (1917). Zone Therapy: Or, Relieving Pain at Home. This is the foundational text where William Fitzgerald introduced his "zone therapy" approach.
- Ingham, E. (1977). Stories the Feet Can Tell. A key text on reflexology that expanded upon Fitzgerald's zone therapy, especially focusing on foot reflex points.
- Buczynski, M. (2015). Reflexology: Health at Your Fingertips. This book provides a modern perspective on reflexology and zone therapy, integrating them with contemporary wellness practices.
- Edwards, S., & McFerran, P. (2011). The Effectiveness of Reflexology in Treating Chronic Pain: A Meta-Analysis. Journal of Alternative and Complementary Medicine.
- Jones, M., & Reed, P. (2007). Energy Medicine and Healing: A Critical Review. Journal of Alternative and Complementary Therapies.
- Oschman, J. L. (2000). Energy Medicine: The Scientific Basis.
- Radin, D. (2006). Entangled Minds: Extrasensory Experiences in a Quantum Reality.
- Ernst, E. (2009). The Efficacy of Complementary and Alternative Medicine: A Review of the Evidence. Journal of Clinical Epidemiology..
- Cummings, T. M., & Martin, J. L. (2008). Reflexology: A Critical Review of the Literature. Complementary Therapies in Clinical Practice.

- Kaptchuk, T. J. (2000). The Web That Has No Weaver: Understanding Chinese Medicine.
- Anodea Judith (2004). Eastern Body, Western Mind: Psychology and the Chakra System As a Path to the Self.

Glossary

Acupressure

A traditional Chinese medicine technique that involves applying pressure to specific points on the body to promote healing and relieve pain.

Acupuncture

A practice that uses thin needles inserted into specific points on the body to stimulate energy flow and balance the body's natural systems.

Aromatherapy

The use of essential oils from plants for therapeutic purposes, including relaxation, stress relief, and enhanced well-being.

Ayurveda

An ancient Indian holistic healing system focusing on balancing the mind, body, and spirit through diet, herbal remedies, yoga, and lifestyle practices.

Biofeedback

A technique that helps individuals control physiological functions such as heart rate and muscle tension using real-time feedback from electronic monitoring devices.

Chiropractic Therapy

A treatment method focused on diagnosing and correcting spinal misalignments to improve overall health and reduce pain.

Herbal Medicine

The use of plants and plant extracts to prevent, treat, or manage various health conditions.

Homeopathy

A system of medicine based on the principle that "like cures like," using highly diluted substances to stimulate the body's natural healing response.

Hydrotherapy

The use of water in various forms (e.g., baths, compresses, steam) to alleviate pain, improve circulation, and promote relaxation.

Mindfulness

A mental practice of focusing attention on the present moment, often used to reduce stress and improve mental clarity.

Myofascial Release

A hands-on therapy focusing on releasing tension in the connective tissues (fascia) to reduce pain and improve mobility.

Naturopathy

A holistic approach to healthcare emphasizing natural remedies and the body's ability to heal itself.

Osteopathy

A system of treatment focusing on the musculoskeletal system, emphasizing manual techniques to improve posture, relieve pain, and enhance overall health.

Reflexology

A therapy that applies pressure to specific points on the feet, hands, or ears believed to correspond to other parts of the body, promoting healing and relaxation.

Reiki

A Japanese energy-healing technique where practitioners channel energy into the patient to encourage emotional and physical healing.

Shiatsu

A Japanese form of therapy based on acupuncture principles, involving manual pressure on specific body points to balance energy and alleviate discomfort.

Tai Chi

A Chinese martial art practiced for its health benefits, emphasizing slow, flowing movements, balance, and relaxation.

Yoga Therapy

The use of yoga postures, breathing exercises, and meditation tailored to support physical and mental health.

Zoning

A lesser-known therapy focusing on manipulating specific zones of the body (e.g., feet or hands) to influence overall health.